ANAISE RAINE

ISBN 978-1-955156-77-6 (paperback)
ISBN 978-1-955156-80-6 (digital)

Copyright © 2021 by Anaise Raine

All rights reserved. No part of this publication may be reproduced, distributed, or transmitted in any form or by any means, including photocopying, recording, or other electronic or mechanical methods without the prior written permission of the publisher. For permission requests, solicit the publisher via the address below.

Rushmore Press LLC
1 800 460 9188
www.rushmorepress.com

Printed in the United States of America

May you become everything you imagine.

Anaise Raine

Contents

I	Humanity's Memoirs	1
II	29 Remedy Street	3
III	Corner Lady	5
IV	Writer's Confession: Part One	6
V	Dear Leila	7
VI	Statistic	10
VII	Boomerang	11
VIII	Away	13
IX	Toxic	16
X	Choice	17
XI	Game	21
XII	Writer's Confession: Part Two	22
XIII	Obscured	23
XIV	Cycle	26
XV	Divergent Me	28
XVI	To Osman	30
XVII	Break	31
XVIII	Unforeseen	33
XIX	Down Low	34
XX	Something Special	35
XXI	Trade	36
XXII	Writer's Confession: Part Three	38
XXIII	Fade	39
XXIV	Burdened	41
XXV	Memoirs of a Sibling	43

XXVI	Broken	44
XXVII	True to Me	46
XXVIII	Unseen	47
XXIX	Hush	49
XXX	In my time of Dying	50

Humanity's Memoirs

I came looking for shelter, a home away from home,
Fled a poisoned land in hope of finding better.
My village destroyed by famine and greed,
Came followed by a shadow,
Yet I remained so full of light and joy.
All I sought was the dream that was advertised, love and equality.
Progression without prejudice and violence.
How naïve we were to believe such lies,
Evil lurks around everywhere.
Guidance from anyone is all I needed,
Someone to hold my hand.
And shield me from the merciless products of a broken system,
Someone to bring a smile to my face.
Someone, please.
I was denied such a blessing,
Time and time again I was chased through the streets,
Unable to understand why.
Undeserved hatred by aimless youth.
How can I blame them?
Minders looked on, condoning violence.
And letting immorality fester,
Neglecting their duty to guide and teach.
Raising a generation corrupt at the core,
Like those before them and those before them.
Mama pleaded and pleaded for assistance,
Power belongs to the privileged.

Had she been someone else,
They would've taken notice and acted.
Needless to say, my suffering was ignored,
For I am part of the historically disenfranchised and prosecuted.
Glimmers of hope shone and called to me,
Refuge I sought in those older.
For they refused to let me be ignored,
And saw how my eyes sparkled with elation.
Saw behind how disorientated I was,
Saw beyond what I wore on my head.
In many ways, I represented so much.
Hope for a better life for my people,
And uncorrupted youthful glee.
Oh, how I wonder what I would've been?
A mother? A wife? A scholar?
I'm forever left to wonder.
As I struggled to breathe,
One thought coursed through my body.
Had I been someone else,
Had I been a different girl,
Would I be drowning in this river of oppression?
May I forever be remembered.

29 Remedy Street

I often watch from under the trees,
Little girl living my dream.
Someone to thrown her in the air,
Someone to buy her ice cream.

Strangers pass by,
One uncomfortable glance my way.
Void of any responsibility,
Sympathy won't make it okay.

I watch as she's protected from the cold,
And the dark.
I look on as she's loved unconditionally,
The difference is stark.

Days bare no meaning,
Time a distant friend.
Every performance and every recital,
She has someone to attend.

Passed around like someone unwanted,
Saw others alongside me get adopted.
She never has to worry or to feel scared.
A couple of protectors, all of my pain she is spared.

In every institution,
Someone took advantage.
A little girl with no one,
Unimaginable damage.

Behind closed doors,
Everyone turned a blind eye.
No power. No choice to comply.

Her first lover comes by,
A father to warn him.
Could not speak out,
Future for us was always grim.

Years went by before he paid for his sins,
Too many years too late.
For me, he had sealed my fate.
I see his face etched into the bins.

At 18, she leaves to make herself a career.
At 18, I was a broken girl who had to disappear.
Now, I scour the bins for a scrap to eat.
What I would give to be the girl at 29 Remedy Street.

Corner Lady

Day in and day out, I notice her glare.
Not what it seems, corner lady beware.

First time he was full of regret,
He pleaded for us to forgive and forget.

So much love for the old him, I complied.
It happened again; closure I was denied.

Bottle after bottle, a pattern began to appear.
I watched from the shadows, nothing for a child to hear.

My early memories I clung onto dearly,
My mother covered for him so clearly.

Entrapped in my own home, all appeared well.
Put up a façade, not that anyone could tell.

I envy her freedom, no ties to a prison.
I envy her independence, no link to poison.

To the lady at the corner, I would love to meet.
I would rather be at the corner than live in 29 Remedy Street.

Writer's Confession: Part One

I'm a born writer, I swear.
I've got to get it down, it's more than I can bare.
It's eating away at me, claims I'm a liar.
They are just afraid I'm climbing higher.
In between lectures and living, I write.
It's all I've ever imagined, I'm alright.
This is my destiny, I swear it's from God,
I'm going to make it, not for a thick wad.
It all lies underneath, I'm a born writer.
Stay on the straight, always getting brighter.
Keep your eyes open from 6 to 6, don't miss my rise.
I'm a born writer I swear, got to cut my ties.
Got to make the sacrifice to ascend, no tension.
It's my time, make sure you pay attention.
I'm a born writer, I swear.
You despise my talent, shed a tear.
I'm a born writer, I swear.
I'm denying your path, is that clear?

Dear Leila

Longed for it for so long,
One day it all came together.
Made so much better by your presence,
I felt so accomplished.
When we met,
I was crying out for someone,
To come along and be everything I dreamed of,
I was cautioned against such a leap.
Yet I threw it to the wind and leapt.
Now I am in a good place,
Remembering the promise, I made to you,
The Queen alongside me,
Guiding and supporting till the end.
So many would have gave up on me,
Unable to love such a damaged person,
But your love never waivers,
Your beauty never ending,
I am blinded by it.
I am consumed by your grace,
Unable to stop loving you,
To stop you from being my whole world,
Every fibre belonging to you,
Every heartbeat beating to the rhythm of your breath,
I never believed it to be true,
But in the moment, I knew.

She danced like I'd never seen before,
Not particularly skilled,
Bur not weighted by expectation,
Or held down by fate,
Or enslaved by destiny.
She danced like she was the last person in the world,
As if her soul and the ground were one.
Round and round she went,
Never ceasing in energy,
Grinning and spinning,
Bouncing on air. Shaping every particle.
Limbs flowing endlessly.
Restricted by nothing and fearing nothing,
She danced like life itself depended on it,
Roaring her on.
Gliding across a river of emotion,
Wind in her hear and love in the air.
No care in the world.
She knows there's no recipe for love,
No substitute for it either,
Life will never slow down,
The clouds will never stop moving.
She is living in an endless hurricane of action,
And inaction will leave her flailing.
So, she dances to free herself,
Not to impress or impersonate.
Oh, she danced and danced.
Time feared her spirit,
The heavens sought after it.
Oppression was quizzed by her purity,
As if she'd never known him,
Breaking boundaries with every move.

She danced like I'd never seen before,
Eyes glinting as if reflecting a billion stars,
She danced and danced,
Slowly clawing back my sanity.

Statistic

Streets laden with our blood, not theirs
Another pigmented boy, why should they care?
Proving what we always knew,
In their eyes we live a life of no value,
Not saving lives, nor flying planes
Lacking opportunity to chase our goals.
Desperate for a lifeline,
Nothing invested in our communities.
Nothing invested in our future.
We aspire to be greater than our ancestors,
Like they, our hopes and aspirations are subdued.
It's all under a pretence, a claim of equality,
Our children destined to die at their hands.
Their children destined to inherit glorious lands.
Long time since the dark age, there's still no change.
Still very much in a cage.
To them, nothing more than a number.
To them, nothing more than another gravestone.

Boomerang

In the sunlight they sent us out.
Out to fulfil their ambition and greed.
Under the guise of patriotism, we left,
Under a cloud we returned.
We are just shells of our former selves.
Carried it all out as fools,
We dreamt of that which awaited us.
Harrowing images blur into scars,
And scars burn into memories.
We are just shells of our former selves.
The lucky few end up in unmarked graves.
Though we've come far, home remains close.
Horrifying at first, but soon a daily routine.
We are just shells of our former selves.
Nothing seems too far now,
Morality has long been eclipsed.
An honour indeed, we return nonchalantly.
To a life we no longer know.
We are just shells of our former selves.
A medal in exchange for our souls: a fair trade.
Expected to slip back in effortlessly,
After all, we've seen and done,
How can we?
We are just shells of our former selves.
No longer of use; so, we are ignored.
Haunted until submission,

No one recognises anymore.
They leave us to battle alone,
An invincible enemy indeed.
No longer of use to them.
Records erased; hope wiped out.
We are just shells of our former selves.
Left to fight alone, how can we win?
Losing our grip, we do what we do best.
Far from danger, but how are we to know?
Morality has been erased and now we are "monsters".
We are just shells of our former selves.
Young and turned, a result of abandonment.
No one to blame but they who created us.
We can only battle our demons for so long.
Bodies scattered like glass,
Intoxicating smoke all around,
Held it off as long as we could.
People screaming and chaos all around.
Debris and dust settle; the boomerang was always homebound.

Away

There was always something to do,
A place to be or someone to see,
Heart always beating,
To the rhythm of beauty,
I never had to watch as others lived.
Now, I watch on daily,
As people meet their loved ones,
As I once did,
And enjoy a cup of coffee,
Or swap stories of joy and of embarrassment,
Or make plans to make the most of life.
I feel abandoned by society,
Discarded as someone who no longer matters,
Many like me feel the same.
Our voices may have waned,
Our bodies may have declined,
But our souls remain as glorious and proud as ever,
Now tainted with the experience,
And beauty of a hundred years.
In days gone by,
My grief was aided by the company of others,
The lights have dimmed,
The music has died down,
The snow has settled,
And now I'm facing the shadows on my own,
Left to deal with such emotion all alone,

Abandoned by all and remembered by few.
There was a time when I didn't sit alone,
Instead, his warmth and humour sustained me,
And I never felt more alive,
We were meeting our destinies together,
I had every girl's wish.
He never did a crossword without me,
Wherever I was, he wanted to be.
He never made a cup of tea,
Without asking what I wanted,
Or bringing back the biscuit tin.
I was forever at peace with him.
Never felt I needed anyone else.
We watched the world go on,
Knowing our time had passed.
We didn't mind listening to the rain,
As it came down all around us,
Neither did we mind hearing the excited chatter and laughter of schoolchildren,
Filled with such promise.
When he first told me,
I urged him to go,
But he insisted he would be okay,
And I believed in his hope.
Inside me, I knew we wouldn't see the end together,
It made it difficult when the time came.
No one came to see me,
I spent the days watching the seasons change,
Barely living.
Weeks would go by before I saw someone,
Or even heard a voice.
So many out there sharing the same grief,
All alone and away from the world.

I don't want to sit alone anymore.
My soul is dimming at the core.

No fear for myself,
Only watching her watch me.
It killed me quicker than anything else could have,
Sending my mind spiralling with worry,
I only had to watch her watch me.
The clock slowly winding down,
Not long till I bow out,
And I have prepared myself,
But no amount of time could prepare her,
And it's killing me like nothing could ever,
From the time that I saw her.
No words could help her cope,
No sentiment to comfort her,
Just an absent aura,
I could see her unwinding.

Toxic

It is not as easy to understand as easy it is to judge.
She is not healthy for me,
But I fear what will become of me If I cut ties.
Before her, I was spiralling into nothingness.
Despite misconceptions, we feel things too.
At times it may not seem so, but we do.
What will become of me if I let her go?
Can I afford to find out?
Pasta stains and broken glass, been through it all.
Raised voices and neighbour's complaints, do you remember?
Cuts and bruises, late night hospital visits.
Turned my own people against me: I'm forever trapped.
What I quit for her I'm now back to.
I forgave her promiscuity.
She forbade me from living my life,
Now I can't live without her.
It's something I would do all over.
Despite everything I loved her, and I still do,
I could never stop if only she knew.

Choice

Daybreak came and with it his departure.
As fractured as I had become,
I could never let them see,
For I was all that remained.
In time, I began to neglect my own needs,
Sacrificing it all to be there when he decided not to be.
It no longer mattered what I wanted or what aspiration I once had,
To provide and care was my only purpose,
Also taking on the role of someone,
Who valued his own goals above anything and everything.
Evenings came where I came short,
Unable to fulfil my duty and had to make the decision to sacrifice myself for them,
Gladly I would do so every time,
In hope they go onto accomplish unimaginable goals,
And not be blindsided by the ubiquitous injustice.

I was supposed to do what I normally did,
Nonchalantly dashing towards my home,
And that's where I was heading.
Till I received the call.
The given location was familiar to me,
A bustling and busy area.
I knew it wouldn't amount to any good,
Yet I still felt compelled to go,
I felt it wasn't right in my heart,

Being deceitful towards my mother,
And ignoring my instinct to not stray from my safe routine.
Why did I choose to go?
Living in an environment wherein we're forced to value
And protect something which never belonged to us,
And still we shed blood for it daily,
Giving our lives to something so meaningless,
But how are we to see?
Rivalry stemming from supressed anger towards the real problems
Which we lack the means to oppose,
Just the way they like it.
Earlier in the day I'd heard of violence brewing,
The putrid stench of hatred clinging onto the air.
Still I ignored such rumours as I was never one to involve myself in such things.
More time I occupied my time with my true calling: playing the beautiful game.
As I went to change directions by switching buses,
I still felt the feeling in the pit of my stomach.
They never knew any better,
But to target and hunt each other like the inhumane subordinates
They were made to believe they were,
Fixated on tearing each other down.
Despite such a disadvantaged environment there were those like me
That sought something far better,
And I believed we had the makings of that whichever we wanted to be,
Believing humanity would right it's wrongs,
And let us soar higher than we ever dreamt of.
Oh, how we once believed.
As I always did, I read a prayer protecting me in my travels
In manners which God generously provided for mankind.
I peered outside as usual,
Imagining what it would be like to be driving a certain car,
Or to be with a certain girl on the street,

Or what it'd be like to own certain clothes,
I was an avid dreamer like that,
Looking into my future and seeing success.
The cacophony of sound coming from a London Main Street
Blurred into the background as I became entrapped in my own imagination.
All that anyone coming on the bus would see,
As they glided through the upper deck and fell abruptly onto their seat,
Would be a teenage boy with a distant and glazy look in his eyes,
As if he were seeing the endless and fluid prospect that is the future.
I wonder if they'd have noticed the optimism filled pools of honey that were my eyes.
A rapid burst of vibration and I confirmed that I wasn't far out.
Ideally, I could be home before my mother came back from work,
If I came any later, she would drown under endless waves of doubt and worry,
And it pained me thinking about that possibility,
As she's everything to me and in all honesty, she is all I have left,
But if five children were to be left with anyone to care and nurture for them,
She is the one and only.
For so long I'd strive to justify her sacrifice and become everything she'd dreamed me becoming.
Shortly after and I had arrived,
And as I had assumed it was packed with travellers.
I wondered around, constantly searching between the ongoing traffic of people,
Until I saw them opposing each other across the concourse,
Dozens of aimless youths,
Who felt the boy or girl in front of them differed from them because of the different areas they originated from,
Ignoring the very humanity which bound them all.
How could they acknowledge that which they were never taught nor shown?

Panic began to spread,
So, I decided to finally heed my instinct and leave,
But It was already too late for me.
For others it may not be.

Game

They built us up, made us stars.
To watch us self-destruct,
And wreck expensive cars.
Only care about selling papers,
Nothing is off the table.
Endgame is always the same,
Found dead in our homes.
Only so much we can take,
Being punished for being so good.
Talent bringing nothing but punishment,
Trending for a week then we're forgotten,
They move on, onto the next victim.
Same headline, always the same result.
Blame never goes to the ones deserving of it.
This is the life; this is the game.
Why do we matter when there's profit to be made?
Our lives not more valuable than a check.
Dust settles; nothing but an emotional wreck.
So common, this is seen as honourable.
Never addressing the real problem.
This is the life; this is the game.
Young and idealistic, ripe for exploitation.
Death is the price of fame.
Full of hope we were, full of admiration.

Writer's Confession: Part Two

They look astounded, not behind bars.
Always pen in hand, not jacking cars.
I am defying the script they wrote,
And it feels so good.
Lead astray by negative expectations, scared of the hood.
Pretending to care, hatred rooted deep within.
No other path expected to only sin.
Ladder slippery with red rejection, waiting for us to fall.
System rigged to oppress, waiting for us to drop the ball.
Looking after their own, it's their society.
Poisonous emotions filled to the brim with anxiety.
Claims we've come far, still on the same track.
Every avenue is closed by them,
Convinced people of their ideals.
So far gone, it's instilled within,
Total disbelief when it occurs,
As if this isn't what they orchestrated.
Minority opinion shut out, can't say nothing.
Trying to break it all, here goes something.

Obscured

As I lay here shamefully covered in oily chips,
I begin to spiral yet again.
Hypnotised to doubt myself all the time.
Nowhere near the ideal shape,
Changes way out of my control,
Yet I'm taught to blame myself?
So many girls with such beauty,
How could he love a beast like me?
With scars from Manny to Montana,
Does he not see my endless flaws?
Days like today come often where I'm ashamed,
Disgusted with what I see before me.
Tears rain down on me,
Like the endless parade of hate.
I pray and pay for item after item,
Feeding right into their hands,
My fears and self-doubt benefitting the one percenters continuously.
They create doubt to build their mansions,
at the expense of our sanity.
Endless streams of enhanced women plastered on billboards and magazines,
Exposed to oblivious men,
Creating exaggerated expectations
I am pressured to conform to,
Like so many others like me.
Feeling worthless and unwanted,

I consider becoming enhanced.
Again, conforming to an impossible reality.
A vicious cycle indeed.

Her eyes were like something I'd never seen in my whole life,
If only she could see herself through my own.
Still she doubts her beauty,
That's thanks to a hateful society.
She laughed in a way I'd never heard before,
So animated and full of jubilation.
Her glow was as if she was emitting light itself, if only she could see.
Hair as golden as a snitch,
And as quick to bounce gloriously in the air.
Gifted with such drive and energy,
Could put any theory to practice,
Really and truly poetry in motion.
But only if she could see.
Out planting roses and tulips on the Weekend,
Able to show such fondness for the beauty behind the madness.
People have created a world wherein others critique to mask
self-hatred,
And an endless routine of disappointment.
So many lives lost to such a disgraced phenomenon,
Families unaware of youth at war with society's expectations,
To rise above it and find their true calling is a deadly challenge.
Comparing women is an appalling trend,
Immense pain spread with a single tweet.
In closing my eyes, she appears,
Dancing across an endless space,
Vibrating along to the rhythm of life.
Had we not met I'd have never felt hole,
Using clubs to hit on endless women without having a ball.
She has a way of seeing things,
Far beyond for what they really are.

I won't let them tear her apart,
I'll be the saviour she needs to end her tears.
A gift from the heavens she is indeed,
Wrapped and gifted to end my search.
Her warmth could fill an entire home.
And never will I let anyone sell her any different,
But If only she could see herself as I saw her.

Cycle

Hundreds of years have passed,
Ask yourself: what has really change?
A consistent cycle of oppression,
Never really treated as equal,
Equality isn't a gift; it's a right.
Freedom isn't a gift; it's a right.
Justice isn't a gift; it's a right.
How can we thrive and prosper?
As minority are wrongly prosecuted,
And regularly beaten and murdered.
System designed so that crime is what the oppressed turn to.
Lack of opportunities and lack of liberties.
And only their people get in positions of power,
Baton passed from one to another,
They say it's all about who and what you know.
All the minority know is poverty and crime.
Minorities frozen out and left to suffer.
All this feeds into their narrative.
Give the minority nothing,
So, crime is what they turn to.
Killing one another as the corrupt system benefits.
Media love to spread lies,
And paint the minority as evil,
When they are the real evildoers.
They only show people the minority committing crimes and making mistakes.

Where are the mistakes of the oppressors?
Truth is censored and hatred blossoms.
What kind of world do we live in?
People meant to protect and serve are killing,
People meant to lead are spreading negativity.
Minority under the threat of losing their careers,
If they dare speak out and threaten to end the hatred.
Truth hidden from those who seek it,
Following blindly that which they know not.
System designed to judge on the colour of your skin.
Hundreds of years have passed,
But what has really changed?
They are not being kidnapped from their countries,
But still as oppressed as ever.
There are limits put in place,
For the minority to suffer and the white to prosper.
Streets are littered with crime and injustice,
Why do people not see?
The oppressors are dealing with a problem of their own creation.
Treat us all as equals and we prosper,
Give everyone the same opportunity.
Take the minority off the streets and
Give them something to work towards,
Like you do your very own.
Let the truth set everyone free.

Divergent Me

Darling, please be honest with me,
If I wore handcuffs instead of cufflinks,
And wore dreary orange instead of azure blue,
Would you still love me the same?

Darling, please be straight with me,
If I forgot your name every few seconds,
And went from gleeful to spiteful in a second.
Would I still be the one?

Darling, please tell me the truth,
If I called home the local shop's front door,
And not the golden gated residential you're used to,
Would you still tell tales of me to your friends?

Darling, if anything, be frank with me for my own sake,
If I had more peanuts from the brothel,
Then I did pennies in my pocket,
Would you still appease my needs?

Darling, please be honest with me,
If I downed liquor and inhaled every substance known to man,
And you would go days without hearing a word,
Would you still love me the same?

Darling, set the record straight for me,
If I lost the beauty you vowed to love,
And I was just another faceless boy among the damned,
Would you come visit me and grace me with your lavender aroma?

If I were any less the person I am today,
Would you leave me behind in yesterday?
Will you love me even when I decay?
Darling, no matter the circumstance, my love will never sway.

To Osman

How was I to know?
A blissful day so far and no troubles.
Came so quickly; always caught off guard.
Too young for this to happen,
And so, I thought.
So many big moments to come,
And yet you will miss them all.
To die is to cease to exist,
But you always lived in my heart.
Never truly dead.
I am everything you wanted me to be.
But you will never know.
Never will I get to look after you in old age.
I stood at my wedding making my toast,
And looked out expecting to see you.
I held my child and turned to introduce you.
In your memory I told him stories of you.
I got promoted and called to let you know.
Time and time again I reach out to a ghost.
You were always around when I needed you most.
Needed help with my proposal,
But you weren't around to guide me.
Your beloved Red Devils won many trophies,
And you never got to see.
It's only now, as I lay here dying,
I realise through me; you were there for every moment.

Break

Fear of abandonment and fear of rejection,
He can't even admit it to himself.
How long can he keep it inside?
Subduing his true self,
The pain will always be a part of him.
Already ridiculed and ostracised,
He can't afford to be even more different.
Name after name, he will always remember.
All he wants is that which others have found.
His passion is no different than anyone else's,
Yet he still remains trapped.
Barely clinging onto hope,
This isn't a life for anyone.
Deep inside he is full of emotion and passion,
Untapped yet still as prominent as ever.
So far from a just life,
So far from a fulfilled life.
Living with a shadow around his heart.
Let him be free and let his heart be clear.
Feat pounding the pavement,
Lungs gasping for air; he ran.
Not knowing where, he ran.
Aim was the same as always,
Avoid the group and avoid the agony that'd ensue,
The moments of avoiding eye contact with parents,
Hiding the blue behind layers.

Blustery wind brining more tears,
A mind in a forever limbo of panic,
Already difficult to accept himself,
Adding to that would tip him over the edge into nothingness.
A corner turned,
Rain joining in on the fun,
Feet beginning to soak,
Backpack filled with dampened notes,
Proud artwork lost to senseless acts.
A rare glance back and hope visited,
Hand on knees,
And a rare break.
All for following the wishes of his heart.

Unforeseen

Calendars and schedules; so much planned ahead.
No thought as to the end, too much left.
Time passes, getting closer to the edge.
Birthdays and bar mitzvah's, no faith in destiny.
Never stop to reflect, blazing through every moment,
Where are we heading?
Rash decisions and selfish insolence,
There's never any afterthought.
Sensitivity and self-reflection are ridiculed,
No idea if there is a purpose to all the sacrifices we make.
And when we are put before him,
How will we explain our ignorance?
Time and time again, we were warned as those before us were warned.
We were told of the consequences of their disbelief,
Yet we hath ignored the guidance we were blessed with.
One day, we will come to regret the message we mistakenly did not heed.
We lack the foresight to see our path,
So, a path was signposted for us.
Yet we have turned a blind eye to the sign.
Only In retrospect will we see our crime.

Down Low

Seems like a point of no return, lost it all.
Too much at once, pass the pills.
Gave it all she had. No order too tall.
All came crumbling down, ran for the hill.
Words of the forgotten girl, all purpose is lost.
Gave It to him, came at a great cost.
They ponder my naivety; he wasn't always a monster.
Heart is broken, one huge blister.
Contemplated meeting grim early,
All the loneliness has consumed me,
I want to make it all stop; I see so clearly.
No one understands, they say let my crazy be.
Going to become another statistic.
Only time I actually matter and belong,
Looking at me, everything appears fantastic.
In those times, drowning in song.
In death there's no more loneliness,
Alongside the forgotten, there's no melancholy.
Molly got me feeling so numb, full of emptiness.
The darkness and I are one, not so jolly.
No one will notice my absence.
At least I left with a clear conscience.

Something Special

For so long, I have been longing for something special,
To appease the empty space in my heart.
In all honesty and heart, I preach to you,
Since I was bestowed with the knowledge,
Of what true love is and how your feet dazzle on the bewildering clouds,
When such feeling enlightens the halls of your spirit,
I have yearned for such feeling explicitly but to no success.
Such completeness has and will forever perplex me.
I'm waiting for something special. I wait on.
I would be betraying your endless trust in me if I declared,
That I have never acclaimed to possess such feeling.
When I relay such frustration to the heavens,
I am advised to attain patience first-hand,
In virtue I must be to appease the creator,
But till such blessing befalls me, I must yearn for something special.
The wise long for what others only dream of attaining,
The fools are content with what all possess, and all are content with.
Thus, I still find thyself at this predicament.
When I attain what I long for, I will notify you first and foremost.

Trade

My perception is so altered,
I am never to know what problem I could face in any day,
Every error is so highlighted,
Every mistake so public,
They feel they made me,
So, I am to do with as they please,
Leading people to believe in someone that is not remotely me,
Hard to maintain a healthy mind,
Surrounded by parasites,
I am only a tool they can use,
To further their ambitions.
So difficult to see who is being genuine,
Even those I knew to be,
I began to doubt as well.
It was not always like this for me,
Began out loving the freedom of expression,
Mesmerised by the attention and never-ending appraisal,
But I could not be allowed to have it all without submitting,
And becoming their poster boy,
My dream could have ended so differently,
If I could live freely,
But everyone who enters this snake pit of an industry,
Knows you have to trade a piece of your soul,
I only wish I did not have to.

Pinned to the very corner,
Almost as if we were all trying to avoid attention,
But desperately failing.
Trying to remember why I even agreed,
Feeling very out of place,
It was not something I'd ever do on my own.
Round and round the lights went,
Pressuring people to go on,
And try to impress the crowd.
Most succeeded at only providing laughter,
All was well till that dreadful moment,
Dazzling lights zooming onto you,
Caught by surprise as the cheers roll on from around you,
As you stumble on,
Sweat pouring from every pore,
Blinded by the lights,
The weekend crowd buoyed by my wide-eyed expression,
Instantly I faced down to avoid the intense
Yet curious glares I felt.
Somehow, I stumbled through a line,
Looked out, expecting laughter but was only met,
With a shocked murmur,
So, I continued,
I closed my eyes to feel calmer.
To feel connected to a higher form of expression.

Writer's Confession: Part Three

Accepted their place in it all,
Natural for them to envy your aspirations.
Mocked for hoping, mocked for dreaming.
Believe in my vision, believe in my talent.
Not where I'm supposed to head,
Only have one chance to live,
Might as well live my own way.
Shady path needs to maintain a balance.
Don't want to alienate the ones who care,
Hard to see where I'm going,
Know I'm not here yet.
Want to settle like the majority do,
Can't shake the aspirations.
Haunted by imagination.
Wish it were someone else,
Know I'm not supposed to think it.
I didn't choose it, it chose me.
I'm a born writer, I swear.
It's more than I can bare.

Fade

I can only imagine how I'll get through,
There was a time I lived with certainty,
Knowing I would make every breath count,
And I know I did.
My little girl is constantly around me,
Reminding me what I have long lost,
The devilish sparkle of a young soul,
Entwined with a never-ending belief in the future.
She glared quizzically into my eyes,
And I could only imagine what she saw,
For they no longer glow as they used to,
And are haunted with an eternity of loss and wear,
Never given a break, never given freedom.
I refuse to stare too long into hers,
For fear of tainting her soul,
For it is too late for me.
I gesture for her to not look too long.
As the holidays come and go,
I can feel it giving away,
Becoming a part of something else,
Soon I won't notice anymore,
I did not need to be told,
By people in white jackets.
There are some I wish would go first,
Too many to count,
But I know those I would let go,

Leave myself with my most treasured memories.
It is only fitting that this be how I meet my fate,
My mind was beginning to weigh heavy,
An uncontrollable tape,
Playing constantly at the forefront,
With or without my consent,
Losing control,
Some parts bought a faint smile to my face,
Some made my eyes go dark,
All tied a hefty anchor that's slowly weighing me down.
I can only hope to be cured by watching her collect her own memories,
As mine continue to depart me,
Writing is all that helps me,
My journal an endless collection of notes to myself,
Reminding me of the simple things.
Go to the store, mop the floor.
My poems, a plethora of emotion,
Tied to the years of memories.
I got through one last one with difficulty,
Knowing soon there'll just be a shell left.
I hope, in leaving her these writings,
She can finally look into my eyes.
I'm content with every memory I made,
I can now watch myself fade.

Burdened

Constantly worried and looking forward,
Always wondering what'll become of me,
Coming from where I'm from,
Definition of success is warped,
Survival is the only goal.
There's constant pressure to redefine success,
Not for myself but for others after me.
Pressure to become something greater.
Burdened since I was born,
I've never really known any better.
So many gave so much,
Even to just have a chance.
Barely living as I'm looking ahead,
All this anxiety is starting to define me,
I feel as troubled as ever.
Stacked odds are a familiar notion,
Chances are slimmer than ever.
Being a visionary is my gift,
Will it be enough?
Will it deny those who wish to confine my people to this life?
As if carrying my own hopes and dreams wasn't enough,
A beacon for so many to believe in.
I envy those without such burdens.
My successes will only be substantial,
When I see them celebrate.
My path is set out before me,

I don't have the luxury of choice.
Filled with insatiable desire,
I'm forsaken. I'm plagued.
Forever sinking.
Oh, I'm so burdened.
Can no one see?
Can no one believe in me?

Memoirs of a Sibling

My Dearest Brother,
If only you knew the agony writing this brings me,
Seems only yesterday we ran around the house,
But so much time has passed by since we
Jumped gleefully on the trampoline.
Being this close to the edge hath made me,
Relive every memory and every smile.
I'm at peace lying on the bed as my body fights itself.
Those that once knew me have moved on,
I'm watching from the side-lines as they reach milestones,
I was on course to reach and love as I was destined to love.
Your love has never abandoned me even in this weakened state.
I love you the more in that I believe you had
Like me for my own sake and for nothing else.
To feel nothing would be a welcome mercy.
Yet I have so much more to experience,
So much more to share with.
I don't want you to jump alone.
Will I ever come home?

Broken

All this outrage and support for the movement,
But where is the love for countries in constant suffering?
Media using misdirection to conceal the truth,
Shed light on the death and destruction,
Is that too much to ask them?
Give the people a chance to show their humanity.
Give the people a chance to show their love.

From young they instil false ideals,
Showing us fact after fact,
Teaching us to follow and not lead.
They teach us about poverty and oppression,
Instead of love and freedom.
No room for creative thinking,
Wanting us to follow corruption without blinking.
They groom us to follow a certain path,
Those that diverge are left to the streets.
Pushing us to spend lifetimes behind desks,
Feeling hollow inside and oppressed.

Few ethnic minorities that rise against the system succeed,
And if they do, their success is capped.
Try to stand up and old mistakes mysteriously resurface,
Destruction of their character is the norm.
Society poisoned with lies and greed.
Oppressors believe money makes them exempt from the laws of the land,

Taking advantage of the young and idealistic,
Too afraid to speak up and breathe.
Scars leading to addiction,
Memories leading to a lifetime of sorrow.
It's just emotion.

True to Me

In the dunia, so easy to be another lost soul.
Drowning in thick envy, so easy to be a troll.
Mainstream poison shapes the young minds,
No idea where to go, stuck in binds.
Chasing what they convinced us is success, face on every paper,
They left something out, not any greater.
Built up ideals, poison in our veins.
Still living in a backwards thinking society, they got the reins.
Endless negativity seeping in, no one is the wiser.
Read carefully, the pen is mightier.
No surprise, society ripe with misdeed.
No surprise, they are following the wrong creed.
True to me, it's a thick wilderness.
True to me, trees covered in sickness.
Stay true to the colourful wilderness that's your heart.
Never let your independence depart.

Unseen

She was blinded by lust,
Letting it drive her search,
Unsurprisingly it led to someone undeserved,
If she could see with heart,
She would notice what she longed for was right here,
Not standing out as much,
But still very much there,
Hoping for a miracle to unveil him to her.
Instead, she sought the ever apparent,
As they always do in time,
And such consequences were predictable,
But if only she could see.

I could never be the one,
Passed and always overlooked,
Onto the more apparent choice,
So many lonely nights ending in a wet pillow,
Bloodshot eyes peering into the abyss of the night sky,
Heart heavy with self-loathing and doubt,
It's always a solemn cloud of sorrow.
Following me around,
Not allowing me to believe in a miniscule of hope.
Unable to loosen the noose,
Of societal prejudice based on image,
Constantly told it's in my imagination,
Made to feel even worse,

As I begin to doubt what I believe to be true.
And I know it'll be the end of me,
But at least I'll finally be able to feel true liberty,
Only respite I know will be in passing.
I'm always envisaging it in my head,
Living in this seamlessly free land,
An escape from the endless seam of misery,
It's all in my head apparently,
If only they knew.
No one talking the time to see beyond
What they're told is the norm,
Afraid to confront a "distorted" reality,
Afraid to address a deep-rooted problem.
How do I remain optimistic?

Hush

Promotions and opportunities,
All comes with a price for her.
So naïve to think it was due to effort,
No, it's due to her figure.
It doesn't need be so hush.
Violated in front of so many,
All their eyes hit the floor.
Can't act if you don't see,
Defenceless like others before her.
It doesn't need to be so hush.
If she stands, she stands to lose her career.
Humiliated and oppressed, a damned hierarchy created.
It doesn't need to be so hush.
Robbed of humanity and silence paid off,
Endless compulsive cycle,
Ashamed to call him out; How will they see me?
It doesn't need to be so hush.
She isn't the only one: me too they cry.
Outnumbered everywhere she goes.
So full of troubles and woes.

In my time of Dying

In my time of dying,
I pray to the lord that these words be spoken upon thy tragic end.
If a good fellow is fulfilling his duty to you my lord by blessing my passing,
Thus, time and tragedy have formed an utmost formidable force to acquit thy goodness and service for this world.
For all you who aided me in my trusted path,
I offer the highest order of thy endearment.
My only wish for you is such passing to the above does not acquit you of your duty to the very soil I lay in.
I put my trust in fate and destiny,
The two have driven me to this berth and they shall guide you to God's door.
My dear family, I preach that I stay dear to you even in this ghostly form.
To all I have unintentionally troubled,
Trust that it was not in my intentions and my heart sings in apology for you.
I pray my name is not written in water.
Many setbacks have befallen me, but I strived to forever feed my ambition.
It is only in reflection I realise such ambition cannot be quenched.
To my love, you are the light to my soul, thy hearts entertainer and I could have been put to the sword for you.
One can never truly die,
If he has never really lived,
And unlike so many; I did.

www.ingramcontent.com/pod-product-compliance
Lightning Source LLC
Chambersburg PA
CBHW021451070526
44577CB00002B/366